Dearest Lauren,

Just a small reminder of your home province. Hopefully you'll return to enjoy it with Ash and Craig.

With lots of love

Alastair & Judy

SUNBIRD
PUBLISHING

First published 2003
2 4 6 8 10 9 7 5 3 1
Sunbird Publishing (Pty) Ltd
34 Sunset Avenue, Llandudno, Cape Town, South Africa
Registration number: 4850177827

Publisher Dick Wilkins
Editor Sean Fraser
Designer Mandy McKay
Production Manager Andrew de Kock

Reproduction by Unifoto (Pty) Ltd, Cape Town
Printed and bound by Tien Wah Press (Pte) Ltd, Singapore

ISBN 1-91993-801-X

TITLE PAGE *The mighty Thukela River winds its way from the Northern Berg between Royal
Natal National Park and Giant's Castle Game Reserve, and meanders through fertile foothills.*
ABOVE *The greater doublecollared sunbird (Nectarinia afra) is a frequent visitor to the Berg's aloes.*
LEFT *Clarens sandstone formations cover vast sections of the Southern Berg, which in turn
form part of what is today known as the Little Berg.*
OPPOSITE *The towering Sentinel keeps watch at the northern edge of the uKhahlamba
Drakensberg Park, one of the most multi-faceted of South Africa's World Heritage Sites.*
OVERLEAF *The jagged cliffs of Mponjwane in the Central Berg are separated from the Main
Berg by a chasm 70–80 metres (230–263 feet) wide and 500 metres (1640 feet) deep.*

Introducing the Drakensberg

The Drakensberg range in KwaZulu-Natal is known by locals and those who have, at some time or another, visited these extraordinary mountain peaks, simply as 'the Berg'. Not only does the Berg have a life of its own, but as the cradle of rivers and the birthplace of clouds and rain, snow and even sunshine, it also gives life to an otherwise parched land – and then takes it again! It is also the source of floods that have washed away millions of tons of unrecoverable topsoil into the oceans.

Man has relentlessly toiled to unveil the Berg's enigmas. He has ravaged its resources and destroyed much, but in the end the Mountains of the Dragon remain as indestructible and mysterious as ever. To feel the essence of the Berg, there is no better place than the edge of the summit plateau, watching the sun rise over the far ocean, one gets the feeling of being at the very core of it all.

Magic Mountains of the Dragon

Once a sanctuary for people and entire communities threatened by annihilation and warfare, the Berg has become a 'natural playground in the sky'. Known as *uKhahlamba* – the Barrier of the Spears – by the local Zulus, it is a place of myth and magic that seems to present an ever different, ever more beautiful face.

This awe-inspiring arena has become an oasis for the soul, a paradise for adventure holidays, ideal for the exploring ecotourist, a trendy destination for overseas visitors, and a heaven for intrepid mountaineers. The formidable landscape is covered by a rich, unique flora, and is further brought to life by the numerous animals and birds that have adapted to this region. Standing in the midst of this, breathing in the clean, crisp mountain air, one cannot help but be overwhelmed by a sense of wellbeing and

ABOVE Patches of montane forest flourish in kloofs where streams hurry to turn into rivers as they make their way to the ocean.

happiness. Close by are some of the greatest natural picture galleries on earth – the walls of caves dotted with paintings representing the world of the indigenous San people.

Scientists have proved that the wild, abundant, free-flowing shapes spawned by nature, the glittering waterfalls and the mild warmth of the sun have a great effect on our minds. Walks and hikes in the welcoming sunlight ease the complexities of daily life and smooth away tensions. Smiles come more readily, radiating effortlessly in a universal message of friendliness.

Coming into the Mountains

Most roads leading to the Berg pass through the wide valleys of the KwaZulu-Natal Midlands, also known as the Moist Upland Grassland. The land here is very fertile, with green pastures and umber tilled fields. But, here and there, degradation has set in. In places, the soil is relatively shallow and leached by the rain, and the ensuing erosion has led to the formation of large dongas. Rain is a powerful force here, almost always reaching 1000 millimetres (some 40 inches) per annum. This land, once teeming with wildlife, is now used largely for grazing and crop farming and, in parts, has been entirely transformed into sterile gum,

BELOW Rivers great and small, among them the Mzimkulu and its tributary, carry the waters of the Berg to the Atlantic and Indian oceans.

pine and wattle plantations. The Moist Upland Grassland lies at an altitude of roughly 600–1200 metres (1970–3050 feet), and on the hazy horizon the peaks of the Drakensberg come into view. Dramatic cloud formations often signal the changing climatic zones. In sheltered nooks and crannies, groves of trees flourish – knobwood, buffalo thorn and paper-bark acacias among them.

The valleys narrow out and roads meander along the rivers, while rolling hills become mountains, with basalt-topped fine-grained sandstone cliffs ranging in colour from cream to deep purplish-red with tinges of brown. Once the domain of the San, this area of sandstone cliffs is known as the Little Berg. Here, narrow valleys become ravines and gorges, where green patches of Afro Montane Forests shelter small forest-born plants and creatures that endure the frequent assaults of veldfires, now mostly induced by man. On the steep slopes leading to the plateaus of the Little Berg, you may find the rare Drakensberg protea or the even rarer cloud protea. In fact, this rugged region offers a wide range of habitats and shelters a number of plant communities – despite the relatively shallow, often leached soil, and rocky terrain, particularly around the high peaks that offer shelter to some of the last of the country's lammergeiers (bearded vultures).

ABOVE The dam at the international-standard Drakensberg Sun Hotel offers a host of diverions for outdoor adventurers.

Top of the World

The sun's first rays strike the jagged teeth of the Escarpment so that they take on an almost blood-red glow – an early-morning tribute to *uKhahlamba*. It is relatively easy to reach the lofty peaks above 3000 metres (9850 feet), where streams form the head-waters of South Africa's major river systems, including the Thukela and Orange, as well as the Mkhomazi and Mzimkulu.

It is on the summit of these towering buttresses that you can almost touch the clouds. Vultures glide past, a brook – just born – sparkles brightly as it rushes by, eager to plunge down the Escarpment. This world is pure joy – until the dark clouds pile up and are soon ready to burst and feed the streams and rivers and the land lying east and west.

The Mont-aux-Sources, at 3282 metres (10,770 feet), is not for nothing known as the Mountain of springs, for this is the birthplace of the dry country's most important rivers. Up here it is easy to cross infant streams and it is hard to believe that these will merge to become the mighty Orange, which travels more than 2000 kilometres (1240 miles) westward before plunging into the Atlantic. The Thukela ('The Startling One') follows a shorter route and travels only 320 kilometres (200 miles) to the Indian Ocean, but remains South Africa's largest river by volume.

To appreciate the grand splendour of it all, allow the eye to roam from the Escarpment of the Amphitheatre, taking in the spectacular mountain scenery, from towering, craggy peaks over sandstone cliffs, down to the sweeping grasslands at the foothills where calming, pebble-strewn streams and cascading waterfalls cut through indigenous forests. High above, in the deep blue sky, the rare and beautiful lammergeier, the majestic black eagle and the speedy lanner falcon ride the winds.

While numerous short walks end at secluded shady spots, waterfalls or in open meadows with rich patches of indigenous flowers, longer hikes may lead deep into unspoilt wilderness areas, to hidden caves and overhangs where the San people used the fine-grained sandstone as their canvas. In fact, it would indeed take a lifetime to discover all the treasures of the Berg.

ABOVE Visitors intent on some high-tech hiking through the Berg may be air-lifted to a ledge near the top of Cathedral Peak.

But the mighty mountains are not just a playground for city folk. Those who live in its shadow struggle to survive. The Berg has not been able to attract the wealth that is necessary to help develop impoverished local communities.

ABOVE The famed Cascades are probably one of the most highly rated viewing spots in the Royal Natal National Park.

ABOVE Extreme poverty mean that locals make do, using sun-baked adobe to build an outhouse in the foothills of the Cathedral range.

Made of Fire and Water

The Drakensberg range differs from all other alpine mountains around the world. While most have been shaped by tectonic uplift, the Berg was created by erosion working at the edges of the Southern African Highlands. The eastern rim roughly parallels the southeastern coast of South Africa and extends for approximately 1100 kilometres (685 miles) from the Great Olifants River in Limpopo Province to the mountains of the Stormberg in the Eastern Cape. But the Escarpment reaches its greatest height and splendour along the borders of KwaZulu-Natal and the Kingdom of Lesotho.

It all began more than 500 million years ago with deposits of sandstone, mudstone and shale on the floor of ancient oceans, which in turn became huge warm-water lakes filled with sediment. This is where the first dinosaurs left their footprints. Many aeons later, when the southern continent of Gondwana broke up, masses of basaltic lava were freed from the bowels of the earth and overlaid ancient sedimentary rock formations.

Part of the eastern region of southern Africa is covered by layers of basalt of up to 1.5 kilometres (1 mile) thick and interspersed with outcrops of dolomite. A slight tilt towards the Indian Ocean in the east serves to smooth the progress of erosion, while basalt and sandstone crumble under the pressure of sun, wind, water and ice. At the same time, torrential floods continue to hurl their debris towards the Indian Ocean, as they have done for thousands of years, still shaping the gigantic Escarpment, which influences both the weather and life of the entire subcontinent, creating and sustaining the monumental landscapes, as well as a rich flora and fauna. The Escarpment thus still retreats steadily in a westerly direction at a rate of about 1.4 metres (4½ feet) every thousand years.

The Source of Life

'The original principle of all things is water, from which everything proceeds and into which everything is again resolved.' These are the wise words of the Greek philosopher Thales of Miletus (*circa* 625–546BC), considered one of the 'Seven Wise Men of Greece'. Without water we would not be. Water also shapes what we today experience as the wonderful world of the Drakensberg, where porous soil and indigenous vegetation still keep the water clear and healthy.

In the Drakensberg – as it is everywhere else on Earth – the never-ending hydrological cycle, driven and regulated by the sun, begins with tiny water droplets, which form the massive clouds that frequently shroud the Escarpment. The fate of such a droplet is truly unpredictable. It might hang in the air for days, as mist or cloud, before it reaches the earth as rain, snow, hail or dew. It might feed a river or remain for months or even years in one of the tarns on the slopes of the Berg. It might help to replenish the mountain wetlands or sink underground, or be absorbed by roots or thirsty plants, swallowed and then perspired by human beings or animals. But, at sometime or another, the droplet will resume its journey as part of a torrent or a stream, which will eventually feed into the big rivers and thus become part of the most important watershed of southern Africa, spilling into two separate oceans.

ABOVE Rural communities cling to traditional custom, and the iSangoma will process the snake and leguaan skin into potent muti.

In fact, South Africa, which is mostly arid or semi-arid, would probably be a desert if it were not for the Escarpment rim on its eastern flank, which provides a huge share of the country's water requirements. The Drakensberg is probably the best watered and certainly the least drought-prone area of southern Africa.

ABOVE A keen sense of entrepreneurship has seen the workers of the farm Tevreden near the Mnweni range turn to cheese-making.

Major Ecological Communities

The extensive ecological communities of the Drakensberg range belong to one of the great grassland regions of the world, known locally as the South African Grassveld. Fire, frost and grazing ensure the maintenance of its structure and its extremely high biodiversity. This major biome is the most threatened ecological community in South Africa, yet grassland is one of the most ancient vegetation types in the world and once covered more than 50 per cent of the African landmass. Today the higher regions, most notably the uKhahlamba Drakensberg Park, are the last vestiges, and the most important, of the less than 2 per cent of South African Grassveld under full protection.

As the view changes with the altitude, so do the typical plant communities. These fall into three separate vegetation zones, defined according to altitude, and comprise the Afro Montane Grassland at 1200–1700 metres (3950–5600 feet), Afro Mountain (or subalpine) Grassland at 1700–2600 metres (5600–8500 feet), and High Altitude (or Alpine) Grassland at 2600–3480 metres (8500–11,400 feet).

Montane belt plant communities are extensive and extremely rich in species diversity. Tree ferns, for example, thrive in moist conditions, while spreads of bracken fern provide cover for many small creatures, and proteas host spectacular bird and insect life during the flowering season. While the protea prefers the drier north-facing slopes, most of the remaining Afro Montane indigenous forests – also called Subtropical Montane Cloud Forest – found here generally face south. They shelter in moist, frost-free kloofs and ravines with abundant water, where veldfires do not reach. Stately trees, such as the yellowwood, are surrounded by fire-resistant plants on the forest margins, which shelter bushbuck and common duiker.

The Afro Mountain Grassland, on the other hand, includes the spurs of the Little Berg, where subalpine fynbos grows surrounded by dominant grassland. Grass covers most of the steep-sided spurs, which stretch away like huge tentacles from the Escarpment at an angle of about 90°. They are probably the

ABOVE *The mood of the Berg may change in a flash from tranquil and benign to dark and menacing and many a peaceful day ends with thunderous discord. A storm brewing over the Cathedral range in the late afternoon is reminder indeed of the volatility of the Berg's temperament.*

leftovers of a once mighty escarpment wall and free-standing peaks, initially carved out of the wall by erosion. These spurs are part of the Afro Mountain Grassland, which covers an altitude of roughly 1700–2600 metres (5600–8500 feet), where it is hit by summer rains and thunderstorms. Typical for this region is the distinct tinge of the red grass *Themeda trianda* in autumn and winter.

The High Altitude Grassland – also known as the Alpine Grassland of the Drakensberg Escarpment – covers the steep, tree-less alpine region of the KwaZulu-Natal Drakensberg and the Maloti Mountains of Lesotho. This region, southern Africa's most important watershed, is marked by towering peaks of up to 3480 metres (11,400 feet), including Mont-aux-Sources, which rises on the western horizon beyond the Amphitheatre. The soils, resting on the massive Drakensberg basalt of the Stormberg Group, are extremely shallow, and are mostly covered by erica-helichrysum heath, tussock grasses, dwarf shrubs, sedge heath, as well as a number of alpine mat-forming and creeping plants. Bogs are common here, and summer rains are well in excess of 1000 millimetres (40 inches), while heavy snowfalls, common in

winter, may occure throughout the whole year. The Alpine Belt is home to only a few animals, notably the ice rat, the lammergeier and a few smaller birds. It is possible, however, to encounter white storks at the top of the Escarpment.

ABOVE *Although ox-driven implements promote erosion, they provide practical means of transport and farming for the people of Mnweni.*

ABOVE Winter winds in the foothills are ideal for motor-less flying, such as hang-gliding from the Ibis Cliffs near Champagne Valley.

Wetland Wonderland

This meeting place of earth and water, vital for life on Earth, is being destroyed at an alarming rate. In the Berg, wetlands range from springs, seep mires and bogs to the alpine wetlands on the summit. A great variety of short grasses and colourful alpine plants are found here and, in fact, thrive in the sodden soil and even the water. Together with those in the mountains of the Rift Valley in Kenya, these form the only true African mires. These bogs and fens feed rivers such as the Thukela and the Orange, which arise on the high plateau of the Escarpment.,

About Fauna and Flora

James Chapman was one of the first travellers to skirt the 'lofty range of the Drakensberg', and in 1849, he wrote: 'The plains for miles around had somewhat the appearance of a living ocean, the tumultuous waves being formed by various herds criss-crossing each other in every direction.' As soon as the hunters interfered,

this ocean quickly dried up until there were more hunters than game. In fact, the white man killed so indiscriminately that '…even the vultures could not devour everything'.

Fortunately, some of the animals returned in time, while some still have had to be reintroduced. Today, the list of creatures found here includes 48 mammal species, about 300 bird, 25 snake and 23 lizard, 26 frog species and subspecies, as well as eight fish varieties. Most of the mammals are seldom seen, except those that boast large numbers, such as the eland (2000+), grey rhebok (1500–2000), reedbuck (1000) and, in the lower regions, small populations of black wildebeest. But the Berg is also home to South Africa's largest populations of the clawless otter and spotted-necked otter. Spotting animals should, however, be considered a bonus, as the main appeal of the Drakensberg lies largely in the overwhelming scenery, the beauty of the wild flowers, its rich birdlife, and the dramatic change in the seasons and unique climate.

The diverse plant life is, in fact, greatly influenced by the equally varied landscape and the effects of soil, climate, drainage and fire. All of this makes the Berg a botanic treasure house with 1677 registered flowering plant species. Five gymnosperms, 72 ferns, and 292 mosses and liverworts bring the total to 2046 recognised species. In fact, scientists have specified over 400 plants that occur only in subalpine and alpine regions, and about 200 of these grow only in the Drakensberg and nowhere else. Dedicated botanists may even find a few more in the river valleys, on the spurs and on the summit plateau.

Wild flower species occur in abundance. Some are famous the world over, like the red-hot poker, agapanthus, aloes, watsonias and gladioli, while others are very rare, such as the threatened blush-pink fire lily.

Campfires in the Sky

Human beings appeared on the scene relatively recently and immediately began to use – and, indeed, misuse – the astonishing resources offered to them. Some lived in awe of the towering

peaks they called *uKhahlamba*. Others, still rooted in European mythology, were inspired by the rugged slopes of the Escarpment to think of the back of a mighty dragon and named the range the *drakensberg* (Dutch/Afrikaans for 'Mountain of the Dragon').

Archaeological sites found in the Berg region date back to the Early Middle and Late Stone Age and are up to a million years old. It is, however, the San who left the deepest imprints. These seminomadic hunter-gatherers belong to the San group and, in all likelihood, made the Drakensberg their home from the Late Stone Age onwards (about 20 000 years ago). In fact, they were probably the first humans to reoccupy southern Africa, after the likes of Mrs Pless and the 'hominids' who provided Africa's missing links. It is estimated that a population of no more than 1000 San lived in the Berg area at one time, but when they were finally wiped out, they left behind a colourful legacy of pictures of themselves, their spiritual life, their surroundings and the animals they hunted, painted in earthy colours on sandstone. About 30 000 individual paintings have so far been counted in the hundreds of caves and rocky overhangs of the

ABOVE Indigenous artists, such as the ceramicists of the Ardmore Studio in the Champagne Valley, have won international acclaim.

ABOVE The early stage of a thunderstorm begins to obscure the sun over the Hlathikhulu wetlands, one of the most important of the Drakensberg region, itself an area widely acknowledged by conservationists worldwide as one of South Africa's most prized natural heritage sites.

Little Berg. Classic collections are located at the world-famous Didima Gorge in the Cathedral Peak area, Battle Cave at Injisuthi, First Cave at Giant's Castle and the Game Pass rock shelter at Kamberg.

The colours used in these ancient wall paintings are those of the natural environment in which the San lived. The iron oxides of the ochre stones around them delivered the reds, oranges and yellows. Black was extracted from charred wood, and white from whitish clay. Blood, fat, water – and even urine – bonded the materials after pulverisation. The artists then used simple brushes made of animal hair, feathers or pieces of bone, sticks or even their bare hands to paint human beings disguised as animals and animals with human features. But, of all the animals of the Berg, none are as prominently portrayed as the eland, which had specific spiritual significance for these early painters. Some rock paintings date back 4000 years or more; others are not even 200 years old and herald the demise of the lithe hunters who depicted the arrival of the white people with their deadly rifles.

Their pictures are not only works of art, but also carry deep meanings, not always fully understood by modern man. They are probably mostly the work of shamans, as we now call their 'problem-solvers', who wielded great powers. The shamans believed – or made people believe – that they were in direct contact with the spirits and deities. During their trance dance, they would tremble, stumble, sweat and bleed from the nose, just like a wounded eland in order to take on the power of the eland. Or perhaps the eland was just a disguise. Their goal was to reach a stage of near-death in order to gain entrance to the hereafter, where they could influence the hunt, the coming of rain, health, birth, death, solve problems between the sexes, establish contact with faraway kinfolk or worship their gods.

These slightly built hunter-gatherers saw the stars as the campfires of their ancestors. Apparently, they also believed in a lesser god, who was perceived as destructive, treacherous and vengeful. It is possible that this lesser god took shape when the Europeans started to settle in the foothills of the Berg. It is clear

that the settlers promptly found their way into the pictures of these skilful painters, but the main body of work centred on animals, forever preserving the creatures with whom they shared this wonderland in the thousands of paintings that still exist on the rock faces of caves and overhangs. Today many of these precious works of art are withering away, due to the power of the elements and the onslaught of vandals.

Lesser Gods?

There is also evidence that Iron Age farmers lived in the foothills of the Drakensberg more than 1000 years ago, and by the late 1600s these cattle herders lived permanently in the area. They were the descendants of the Bantu-speaking people who migrated southward from Central Africa at the beginning of the Christian era. But by 1816, the relative peace of the Berg was shattered by colonial wars and the clashing impis of local groups.

It was in the first half of the 19th century that Voortrekkers and colonial settlers headed towards the soft meadows, deep forests and clear streams of the Drakensberg foothills with their

ABOVE Many caves and overhangs in the Drakensberg offer shelter to overnight hikers exploring the early homes of the San people.

sheep and their cattle, felling the mighty yellowwoods for domestic use, ploughing the land, hunting the eland and interfering with the life of the original habitants.

'Great things are done when men and mountains meet,' claimed the British poet and painter William Blake almost 200 years ago. But the things that happened when men met men in the mountains were not so great. By 1871 the conflict between the settlers and the San had, in a sense, been solved – the entire Drakensberg San population had been wiped out.

The World Heritage site of uKhahlamba

On 29 November 2000, the uKhahlamba Drakensberg Park was proclaimed South Africa's first combined Natural and Cultural Heritage Site – only the twenty-third such park in the world. The uKhahlamba Drakensberg Park, stretching for about 200 kilometres (124 miles) from north to south, covers more than 2400 square kilometres (243,000 hectares) of largely untouched wilderness areas. Today, it serves to protect not only these unique landscapes, but also the artistic legacy of the San people and the wealth of flora and fauna characteristic of the region.

ABOVE The cottages at Didima camp, ideal starting point for explorations into San country, were built to resemble a San cave.

A group of forward-thinking individuals has almost completed the arduous task of stringing the pearls of the Berg together into a sparkling diadem. The many greater and smaller nature reserves on the South African side, including the Royal National Park in the north, Giant's Castle in the Central Berg and Cobham in the south, as well as other pristine wilderness areas have been linked together into one great conservation belt.

Justification for the Park to be declared a World Heritage Site is based on four principal attributes:

Firstly, the Drakensberg is an outstanding example of an escarpment mountain formation where a continuous process of erosion has exposed a 200-million-year-old geological sequence of sandstone, shale and basalt.

In addition, it is a major component of the Afro-Montane biome, and therefore has unique altitudinal-zoned vegetation communities of high plant diversity, from the alpine-tundra flora at high elevations to the lower-lying grasslands, as well as a great diversity of wetland types.

Also, some 190 plant species occur only in the Park, as well as 35 amphibian, bird and mammal species that are endemic to the South African Grassland and Montane region.

Finally, the Park contains some 600 rock shelters in which over 35 000 individual images painted by San hunter-gatherers are found. This is the richest San rock-art area in Africa and possibly the richest rock-art centre in the world.

Peace Park: Nature without Bounds

Transfrontier nature conservation has become a necessity, an acceptance that nature knows no man-made boundaries, and the Maloti-Drakensberg Project – the envisaged Peace Park – is literally taking this idea to new heights. The Drakensberg and Maloti form an alpine and Montane belt with breathtaking mountain and river landscapes, matchless biodiversity, vital water resources and priceless ancient cultural monuments, said to be second to none in the world. All this has for a long time been under immense pressure by human beings and their livestock.

ABOVE Natural pools and tarns protect the Berg's specialised aquatic life. Some even shelter adapted fish that can survive dry spells.

Cross-border management could, therefore, bring much-needed relief. Planners have concentrated on a 300-kilometre (186-mile) stretch arching from Mont-aux-Sources in the north to the Eastern Cape and landlocked Lesotho in the south. The proponents of this ambitious project seem to have their work cut out to preserve at least the most important parts of this immense stretch of mountainous country, about 70 per cent of which is in Lesotho and most of the remaining 30 per cent part of South Africa's uKhahlamba Drakensberg Park. They also dream of having it declared a World Heritage Site.

A major stumbling block in the quest to protect the region's water, wilderness and wildlife is the fact that conservation is hardly a priority in impoverished Lesotho, where only about 0.4 per cent of the land is protected – the lowest rate in the world. Therefore, before this monumental dream can be realised, the quality of life of the mountain people on both sides of the border will have to improve considerably before the citizens of Lesotho will be able to fully appreciate the need for nature conservation.

Enigmatic Peaks

While KwaZulu-Natal's Drakensberg mountain range is world famed for its towering peaks, such as Champagne Castle, Giant's Castle, Cathedral Peak and Hodgson's Peak, a surprising number of the peaks of the High Berg – some celebrated, some notorious – are still little known. In fact, some have not even been named yet, although it is true that mountaineers have indeed conquered them all over the last 100 years or so. Most of these are, however, not strictly 'peaks', but rather elevations of the walls of the Great Escarpment. Among the 'freestanders', which can be viewed from all sides, are some of southern Africa's most majestic: the 3165-metre (10,385 feet) Sentinel, the 3047-metre (10,000 feet) Eastern Buttress, 2871-metre (9420 feet) Mount Ompie, 3004-metre (9856 feet) Cathedral Peak, 3149-metre (10,332 feet) Cathkin Peak, 3051-metre (10,010 feet) Rhino Peak, and the Outer and Inner Mnweni Needles, which are 2890 metres (9482 feet) and 2905 metres (9531 feet) respectively.

BELOW The wide-ranging African gladiolus or Natal lily occurs in different colour forms, which flower at different times of the year.

ABOVE Free-ranging horses celebrate their freedom at a stud farm near Eliot in Eeastern Cape, where the mountains of the Drakensberg range come to an end in a display of wonderfully bizarre sandstone formations that form a spectacular backdrop to the province's northern regions.

The most famous of all is probably 3234-metre (10 610 feet) Monk's Cowl, sharp and pointed, almost sinister, and the scene in January 1938 of the first fatal climbing accident in the Berg. Two South African mountaineers were the first adventurers to attempt to reach the top of Monk's Cowl from the base camp under the Cowl. During the final assault of the sheer rock face of 120 metres (394 feet), one of the climbers lost his hold, pulling his partner, to whom he was tied, with him. Both came to rest about 60 metres (197 feet) below and were emerged relatively unscathed – until one lost his footing and plummeted to his death. Their route was finally mastered in 1962.

In fact, most of the peaks of the magnificent Drakensberg have some kind of local myth, urban legend or dramatic story – some famous, others still a secret – attached to them. Of all these towering sentinels, this is particularly true of famed Thabana Ntlenyana on the Lesotho plateau, at 3482 metres (11 425 feet), four metres (13 feet) higher than the Matterhorn in the Swiss Alps and the highest in southern Africa.

The Climate

Extremes in temperature and high rainfall are characteristic of the Great Escarpment region. As a whole, the climate of the Drakensberg is dominated by a large subtropical system of atmospheric high pressure, marked by circulating winds moving anticlockwise. In the summer months from about November to January, incursions of humid air brought in by the southeasterly winds from the Indian Ocean are quite common. As a rule, rainfall generally occurs in the form of heavy thunderstorms. In winter, atmospheric stability results in a typically dry season, with frost possible during six months of the year. Night-time temperatures can drop to about –20 °Celsius on the summit plateau during winter months. Temperatures vary greatly between night and day and in the different seasons, reaching up to 35 °Celsius during summer on the north-facing slopes. Rainfall is at it lowest during June and July and reaches a monthly average of about 200–240 millimetres (7½–9½ inches) between December and February.

PREVIOUS PAGES The mild December sun over the landmark Amphitheatre quickly eradicates evidence of a summer night's snow blizzard in the high-lying mountains of the Drakensberg.

OPPOSITE The familiar Policeman's Helmet in the Royal Natal National Park provides a fine example of the erosion of local sandstone, clearly capped by much harder basalt.

TOP Many of the more than 1700 plant species of the Drakensberg find their way into the medicine horn of the *iSangoma*, who uses them for their medicinal properties.

ABOVE The deep croak of the guttural toad (*Bufo gutturalis*), seen here climbing an ouhout (*Leucosidea sericea*) tree at the Monk's Cowl camp site, resounds in the still night air.

RIGHT The sparkling waters of the picturesque Gudu Falls tumble over mighty rocks, giving rise to luxuriant greenery that is home to an impressive collection of rare flora and fauna.

LEFT The Thukela River – 'The Startling One' – cascades 850 metres (2 790 feet) in five leaps down the Escarpment, making it one of the highest waterfalls in the world. It has its origin at the top of the Escarpment, where it slowly 'steals' from the Orange River's catchment area, thereby changing the face of South Africa's Great Divide.

ABOVE The horses of Basotho herdsmen – of indefinable mixed heritage and not, as popularly believed, descendants of the hardy Basuto pony – run wild in summer at the top of the Amphitheatre and at other less accessible locales along the summit of the Escarpment.

OPPOSITE Virtually encircled by a series of towering mountain faces, a narrow footpath winds its way from Thendele camp, past Devil's Hoek Valley to the indomitable Policeman's Helmet.

OVERLEAF LEFT As the eye roams over the grassland of the Little Berg, the much-photographed façade of the Amphitheatre is almost dwarfed by an imposing sky that invokes a deep sense of seclusion, solitude and even welcome respite from the fast pace of modern life.

OVERLEAF RIGHT Wildflowers abound in the mountains of the Drakensberg, and nowhere is this more spectacular than in the Thukela Gorge, where a field of bell agapanthas (*Agapanthus campanulatus*) stretches across the mountainside.

Some serious birdwatchers claim that they are able to spot at least 10 per cent of the 350-odd bird species at home in the Drakensberg on a simple day hike from the bottom to the top of the Escarpment. There are, of course, easier ways to enjoy the varied birdlife of the Berg – just sitting in front of your cottage, chalet, caravan or tent or during a short, more relaxing walk.

TOP, FROM LEFT Cardinal woodpecker (*Dendropicos fuscescens*); the endemic lesser doublecollared sunbird (*Nectarinia chalybea*); red bishop (*Euplectes orix*).

ABOVE, FROM LEFT This pied starling (*Spreo bicolor*) was photographed at Sani Top, where it had never been recorded before; pintailed whydah (*Vidua macroura*); the Natal robin (*Cossypha natalensis*)

TOP, FROM LEFT Cape rock thrush (*Monticola rupestris*); narina trogon (*Apaloderma narina*); pygmy kingfisher (*Ispidina picta*).

ABOVE, FROM LEFT Looking more than a little flustered, a small female stonechat (*Oenanthe monticola*) ruffles its feathers to help protect itself from the cool morning temperatures; masked weaver (*Ploceus velatus*); No fewer than nine species of canary (the family Fringillidae, Serinus species) – with their characteristic short, conical bills well adapted to seed eating – live in and around the peaks and foothills of the Berg.

LEFT Almost as an invitation to the daring, a sturdy chain ladder leads from the lower end of the Thukela Gorge to a scrambling path with a view of the Thukela Falls at its end.

BELOW AND BOTTOM Downstream, the Thukela River whirls through yet another gorge, creating ideal conditions for adventurous river-rafting on the wild waters of the Thukela.

OPPOSITE White-river rafting and canoeing under expert guidance is becoming increasingly popular among the many adventure holiday activities offered by the Drakensberg.

OVERLEAF LEFT Of the many Berg experiences, most satisfying is a walk – short or long, easy or difficult – through the varied landscape. This path leads to Basuto Gate and Qua-Qua.

OVERLEAF RIGHT Set against the backdrop of Ploughman's Kop ridge near the Visitors' Centre at the Royal Natal National Park, a little pond covered in a sprawling bed of water lilies provides yet another opportunity to stop and admire the view when exploring the acclaimed national park.

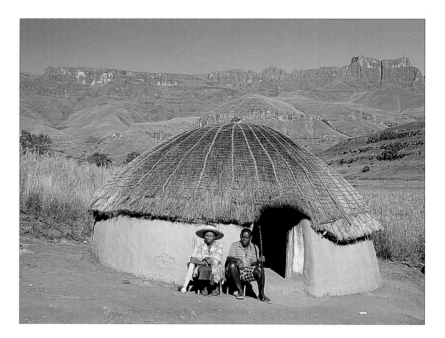

LEFT Many of the women of the Mnweni Triangle in the Drakensberg have developed their basket weaving to a fine art. Selecting the right grass species and drying the blades properly is the first and most important step in a surprisingly elaborate process.

ABOVE Life has not changed much since the amaZizi settled along the banks of the Mnweni, which translates as The Place of the Finger – possibly because of the many naturally occurring pinnacles, pillars, spines and columns for which the area is known. While the pristine landscape of the region is testimony to its rich natural heritage and the enormous potential it holds for the ever-growing tourism industry, only time will tell, however, whether the environment will survive the onslaught of development.

OPPOSITE A blazing field of autumn cosmos forms a jubilant contrast to the still summer-green mountains of the Injati Wall in the Mnweni area.

THIS PAGE, CLOCKWISE FROM TOP LEFT With up to 2000 flowering species, the Drakensberg is richly endowed with striking wild flowers. Still, there remains a number of exotic species from all over the world dotted across the famed mountain slopes. One such species is the beautiful little *Commelina virginica* from the USA, a member of the spiderwort family that is widely cultivated; the beauty contest is nevertheless easily won by South Africa's indigenous star flower (*Hypoxis* sp.); the flower of the pompon tree (*Dais cotinifolia*); the common sugar bush (*Protea caffra*); and the candelabra flower (*Brunswigia* sp.).

OPPOSITE, CLOCKWISE FROM TOP LEFT The bright red Tritonia (*Tritonia disticha*), which may be easily spotted by casual strollers, is used to treat stomach complaints in babies by traditional healers, who know well the tremendous healing powers of Drakensberg flora; the pineapple flower (*Eucomis autumnalis*) is said to help the treatment of fevers and lung complaints; wild orange begonia (*Begonia sutherlandii*) eases heartburn and acts as a protective charm; members of the wild hibiscus species help against bad dreams and internal parasites; *Persicaria* species are used to treat venereal disease.

LEFT Exploring the near-tropical world of the Mlambonja River in Rainbow Gorge remains one of the most popular draw cards to the magnificent Cathedral Peak area.

TOP Although the scenic splendour of this holiday village in the Champagne Valley was, for the most part, created by human hands, it blends well with the natural surroundings.

ABOVE The indigenous landscape of Waterfall Bush in the Sterkspruit valley is an exceptionally beautiful, but little-known grove of mist-belt forest with fine examples of Montane tree species.

OPPOSITE Exploring the terrain of the monumental Escarpment and discovering first-hand the secrets of the Berg – its sights, sounds and smells – is perhaps best done on horseback.

OVERLEAF In summer – when dramatic cloud formations never cease to beguile – the sun often sets in an explosion of light and colour over the peaks and valleys of the Cathedral range.

LEFT, BELOW AND OPPOSITE A stroll through the indigenous forest that lines the eNdumeni stream, with its gurgling waters and gentle waterfalls, provides a gallery of delights to the nature lover. The relatively easy walk to Rainbow Gorge, especially, offers a priceless tranquillity and close-up look at one of South Africa's finest examples of montane forest. Although they cover only small patches of less than 0.5 per cent of South Africa's landmass, montane and lower-altitude mist-belt forests are vital for regulating water resources. They forests are also home to no fewer than 650 plant species, most of which are evergreen. Monkey ropes reach high into the dense canopy, while on the ground shrubs, herbs and wild flowers nourish and shelter wildlife and decaying plant material is converted into rich humus by tiny creatures of the forest.

LEFT The delicate flower of the orchid *Liparis bowkeri* can be used as a love charm – or simply be admired for its extraordinary beauty, on display in its natural habitat: on trees, in leaf litter or on rocks at a height of up to 1 800 metres (5 900 feet).

BOTTOM LEFT A popular gardening flower, the Cape primrose (*Streptocarpus gardenii*), known throughout the world, was already being cultivated in South Africa in the 1800s.

BELOW Various fungus species cling to decaying logs worked over by countless little organisms.

OPPOSITE, TOP LEFT Fungus species are important in the breaking down of plant material.

OPPOSITE, TOP RIGHT The tiny mauve impatiens (*Impatiens hochstetteri*) is another dweller in the damp shade of forests, revealing her beauty only under a magnifying glass.

OPPOSITE, BOTTOM LEFT *Moraeas*, which belong to the iris family, thrive on the forest floor.

OPPOSITE, BOTTOM RIGHT Another common inhabitant of the forest floor are mushrooms. Although many are indeed edible, a number need to avoided by the uninitiated as some can prove fatal when eaten.

LEFT Traditional beehive huts, although not as common as they once were on the slopes of the Drakensberg, are still built according to age-old Zulu custom passed on from one generation to the next. Fortunately, however, traditional handicrafts such as basket weaving are still fairly widely practised, and many of the rural folk rely on their appeal to both locals and, increasingly, international visitors in order to earn a living from their basketry skills.

BELOW The craftswomen of the Drakensberg – and indeed much of KwaZulu-Natal and beyond – boast a variety of weaving skills and offer a wide choice of outstanding pieces. At the same time, it can take several days to finish just one of these huge carrying baskets, and they earn a meagre living.

OPPOSITE Trout fishing is widespread virtually throughout the Drakensberg, but especially in the Southern Berg, such as here at a dam bordering the Mlambonja Wilderness area, where a trout fisherman shoots the line with drag fly on a calm summer morning.

PREVIOUS PAGE, LEFT The vast panorama of the Central Berg incorporates some of the most prominent mountain peaks in the Drakensberg . The flat-topped Cathkin and Monk's Cowl (far left), for example, are linked to the long, almost smooth Escarpment wall, which in turn is connected to the equally impressive Cathedral range. In the foreground are the characteristic flat summits so typical of the Little Berg, while The Saddle (far right) marks the southernmost reaches of the Mnweni range.

PREVIOUS PAGE, RIGHT Standing proudly alongside the instantly recognisable massive hulk of Cathedral Peak (left), the rocky walls of the Bell have seen many a climber scale their perilous heights. While cragsmen have battled to conquer the Bell, a relatively fit climber or hiker may well be able to ascend Cathedral Peak in a one-day return trip without too much discomfort.

LEFT The Sterkspruit Falls have become a favoured spot for day visitors to the camp site near Monk's Cowl, which in turn offers access to a number of hikes and trails in the area.

ABOVE En route to the High Berg, hikers trekking to Blind Man's Corner – notorious for its rapidly changing weather conditions – follow a series of winding contour paths that skirt most of the KwaZulu-Natal Drakensberg range from north to south.

OPPOSITE Although it may take a rather active imagination to make out the form of the mythological figure with the head and breasts of a woman said to be carved from the face of the mountain, the Sphinx remains a well-known lookout point boasting views over the entire Champagne Valley and its surrounding peaks and vales.

OVERLEAF LEFT Clouds above the summer-green slopes of Champagne Castle mark the start of the hydrological cycle that will eventually lead to rainfall over South Africa's most important watershed.

OVERLEAF RIGHT From a viewing point near Vulture's Retreat on the Escarpment, the breathtaking view extends from Cathkin (left) to Monk's Cowl and Champagne Castle peaks. The Escarpment, which reaches right into Lesotho, is, in fact, higher here than the free-standing peaks in front of it.

Birds of prey are numerous in the Drakensberg, from the lowly foothills to the summits of its abundant peaks. The lanner falcon, for example, may often be seen soaring along the richly coloured cliffs of the Little Berg, while other raptors, such as the black eagle, lammergeier and even the Cape griffon (Cape vulture) build lairs mostly in inaccessible places and are rarely seen sailing the skies.

TOP, FROM LEFT Black eagle (*Aquila verreauxii*); African fish eagle (*Haliaeetus vocifer*); and the Gabar goshawk (*Micronisus gabar*).

ABOVE, FROM LEFT Lanner falcon (*Falco biarmicus*); greater kestrel (*F. rupicoloides*); and the secretary bird (*Sagittarius serpentarius*).

While a number of the region's most significant birds of prey are seldom seen, others are spotted fairly regularly at, for example, the famous Lammergeier Hide at Giant's Castle Game Reserve. Others, such as the spotted eagle owl, on the other hand, are heard rather than seen – especially at night at the Mahai camp site. The jackal buzzard and crowned eagle are, however, widespread.

TOP, FROM LEFT Crowned eagle (*Stephanoaetus coronatus*); spotted eagle owl (*Bubo africanus*); and the Cape vulture (*Gyps coprotheres*).

ABOVE, FROM LEFT Lammergeier (*Gypaetus barbatus*); jackal buzzard (*Buteo rufofuscus*); and the Longcrested eagle (*Lophaetus occipitalis*).

LEFT The seemingly endless series of waterfalls, many of them well hidden and still to be discovered, serves to transform the Injisuthi range in the northern reaches of the Giant's Castle area of the Little Berg into a tranquil haven.

ABOVE A lofty homestead at Round the Bend sits atop a hillock in the Bush Reserve, which protects a stretch of indigenous mist-belt forest in the foothills of the Champagne range.

OPPOSITE Morning settles over Cathkin Peak and Sterkhorn, where the the air is clear, the sky blue and only twittering birds – or, perhaps, the raucous barking of a baboon – interrupts the almost devout stillness of the Little Berg.

ABOVE Erosion of the Clarens sandstone in the Monk's Cowl region of Mdedeleo Wilderness of the Little Berg hollowed out the softer parts to create overhangs and caves that once sheltered the San.
OPPOSITE Rangers count vulture populations from Vulture's Retreat atop the Champagne range overlooking the spurs of Cathkin Peak spurs and beyond to the Cathedral range on the distant horizon.

LEFT A small stream, springing from the slopes of Champagne Castle and cascading over the cliffs of the Little Berg, supports an indigenous forest patch on its run to the Injisuthi River.
BELOW A welcoming grove invites explorers to linger for a moment, while the Old Women Stream hurries on through the yellowwood stands near the Injisuthi Hutted Camp where it finally merges with the Injisuthi River.
OPPOSITE At the watershed of the Monk's-Champagne range, one of the highest points of the Escarpment, numerous little streams run in all directions, but all this water will eventually merge and flow into either the Thukela or the Orange River, which has its source nearby.
OVERLEAF The early morning sun immerses the mountain range and the top end of the Injisuthi Valley in a virginal blush. As refreshing as it may appear here, the shaded tarn – a small mountain lake known more commonly throughout South Africa as a *vlei* – may, in fact, disappear entirely during the dry winter season, which sees extremely limited rainfall.

While many of the bird species of the Drakensberg may be dependent on reliable water sources, others have simply become associated with water and do not rely on it as much as one would assume. Some, like the herons, may be found along river courses, but a better bet may be to watch out for them at the numerous dams dotted among the foothills, especially in the Southern Berg.

TOP, FROM LEFT Blackcrowned night heron (*Nycticorax nycticorax*); crowned crane (*Balearica regulorum*); and the South African shelduck (*Tadorna cana*).

ABOVE, FROM LEFT The endemic — and indeed vulnerable — blue crane (*Anthropoides paradiseus*); and the exotic Egyptian goose (*Alopochen aegyptiacus*).

A speciality of the Southern Berg region is the stately wattled crane, a bird entirely dependent on wetlands. Populations of these birds are, however, shrinking rapidly – as are the numbers of South Africa's endangered crane species. The greyheaded gull, usually associated with coastal regions, has now estabished a permanent base at Sterkfontein Dam.

TOP, FROM LEFT Wattled crane (*Grus carunculatus*); and the greyheaded gull (*Larus cirrocephalus*).

ABOVE, FROM LEFT Crowned plover (*Vanellus coronatus*); dabchick (*Tachybaptus ruficollis*); and the African spoonbill (*Platalea alba*).

OPPOSITE Although small streams such as this may, on the surface, seem insignificant, they act as lifelines for indigenous forest patches, and the water flow can be surprisingly powerful, making boulder hopping a lot more demanding than may be anticipated.

ABOVE As if to emphasise the centuries-old landscape of the Drakensberg, the rugged terrain, rocky valleys and densely vegetated slopes are dotted here and there with that plant that is as almost old as the hills themselves – the Drakensberg cycad (*Encephalartos ghellinckii*), seen here in the Cataract Valley of the Injisuthi range.

RIGHT With one small waterfall after another, virtually on every bend in the water courses of the Drakensberg, the rushing water – despite the tranquillity of the vista – is a vital tool of erosion, forever changing the shapes of the Berg.

TOP LEFT San rock art, such as this at Main Cave in the Giant's Castle Game Reserve, is a fragile heritage indeed and is not only vulnerable to vandalism – note the chisel marks here – but also the erosive nature of the elements, as well as, bird droppings, which accelerate the fading of this priceless legacy.

LEFT, CENTRE Part of an exceptionally large eland and other unidentified figures form part of this enormous, natural 'canvas' in Giant's Castle's Main Cave, where the guards who escort visitors to the two principal shelters of the Drakensberg's premier rock-art site provide a running commentary on these ancient masterpieces, providing unique insights into the simple depictions.

BOTTOM LEFT The eland plays a very important role in the ancient mythology and belief system of the San people, and thus feature prominently – in their thousands – in the rock art of the Berg and beyond, along with other large antelope and species with which early inhabitants may have been familiar.

ABOVE. For just a fraction of a second as you turn the corner, this vista may take your breath away – such is the air of ancient mystery in the Berg that you almost believe you have stepped back in time. In reality, the scene is a life-like exhibition of San life, the focal point of Main Cave at the Giant's Castle Game Reserve.

OPPOSITE The so-called Long Panel in the Main Caves is an awe-inspiring spread of just over five metres (17 feet) in length. The details feature two elongated theriantropic figures, mythological characters that are part human and part animal. Above them, to the left, is the fading figure of a feline creature. Despite the mounds of research already conducted into the meanings behind these works of art, much remain unexplained in today's terms.

Opposite, top left *Moraea* species have adapted well to conditions prevalent in the mountain grassland of the Drakensberg.

Opposite, top centre The gnarled Natal bottlebrush (*Greyia sutherlandii*) prefers cliff edges and steep mountain slopes.

Opposite, top right The narrow-leaved sorrel (*Oxalis smithiana*) grows in damp grassland or on rock outcrops.

Opposite, bottom left This two-tiered pelargonium (*Pelargonium schlechteri*) is similar to the Tonga pelargonium, which only grows on sand in Tongaland.

Opposite, bottom right Twinspur (*Discia integerrima*) flowers on cliffs and near streams.

Above Christmas flowers bloom, according to botanists, between October and April throughout the KwaZulu-Natal Drakensberg.

Centre The white-spotted arum Lily (*Zantedeschia albomaculata*) is widespread in damp regions of the Drakensberg foothills and is recommended by traditional healers for its ability to help prevent miscarriages.

Top right Populations of the Natal candelabra flower (*Brunsvigia natalensis*) are unfortunately decreasing due to the draining of marshy areas in the Drakensberg. It is, however, still recommended by *iSangomas* to help straighten the bones of children.

Right *Geranium* species provide a number of well-tried Zulu household remedies to relieve everyday ailments.

LEFT Such is the view of a lammergeier as it circles the Berg between Giant's Castle and the precarious slopes of Sani Pass after heavy snowfall in mid-winter as it searches for the diminutive spoor of eland or other animals. Under the harsh and inhospitable conditions offered by this white blanket, the search for food and shelter is often an unrewarding one, emphasising the unusual hardship and desolation of the 'back of the dragon'.

ABOVE Almost as if in definace of the elements, the steeple of the historic Trapist Reichenau Mission church in the foothills near the town of Underberg points into the grey, snow-laden sky, drawing particular attention to the tiny human settlements in the vast mountain landscape.

OPPOSITE At the height of the bone-chilling winter months, a white desert of snow and ice encircles the tortuous Sani Pass, the highest in southern Africa and the only road access between KwaZulu-Natal and the Mountain Kingdom of Lesotho.

TOP LEFT A sandstone rock in the Giant's Castle range seems to actually glow in the wintry late-afternoon sun. The colours in these rocks have been brought to the fore by the corrosive effects of erosion and the lichens that attach themselves to these boulders – so much so, in fact, that it looks as if the early San artists cleaned their brushes in grand style here.

LEFT The cliffs of the Little Berg at the bend of the Bushman's River guard the two shelters that constitute the Main Caves, used by generations of San people as both family homestead and an exhibition hall on whose walls they have recreated their world for posterity.

ABOVE As it makes its way from its source in the high mountains of the Giant's Castle range, the Bushman's River rushes towards the Thukela River, which in turn marks the southernmost border of traditional Zululand, the lands once reigned over by the mighty Shaka.

OPPOSITE The great basalt block of Giant's Castle mirrors the rays of the rising sun. Celebrated as Alpenglühen (alpine glow) in the Swiss Alps, this natural phenomenon is quite common throughout the northern and southern Drakensberg of KwaZulu-Natal, especially in winter.

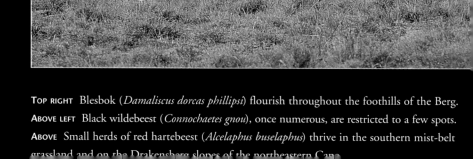

Top left A young female bushbuck (*Tragelaphus scriptus*), a species often seen at the Mahai camp site, browses for selected leaves, fruit, flowers and grazes on short grass.

Top centre A juvenile chacma baboon (*Papio ursinus*) must adapt quickly to the relatively harsh mountain environment, scavenging, hunting and even digging for bulbs.

Top right Blesbok (*Damaliscus dorcas phillipsi*) flourish throughout the foothills of the Berg.

Above left Black wildebeest (*Connochaetes gnou*), once numerous, are restricted to a few spots.

Above Small herds of red hartebeest (*Alcelaphus buselaphus*) thrive in the southern mist-belt grassland and on the Drakensberg slopes of the northeastern Cape.

TOP LEFT While Burchell's zebra (*Equus burchellii*) may be found at a number of places around the southern Drakensberg, mountain zebra are entirely absent from the region.

TOP RIGHT Despite critical decline in the 19th century, substantial herds of healthy eland (*Taurotragus oryx*) have been built up, especially in the central and southern regions of the Berg.

ABOVE LEFT The shy small grey mongoose (*Galerella pulverulenta*) may be seen at Sterkfontein Dam

ABOVE CENTRE The ice rat (*Otomis slogetti*) thrives in the snow and ice at the top of the Escarpment

ABOVE RIGHT The clawless otter (*Aonyx capensis*) eats not only crabs, frogs, birds and insects, but are also regular visitors to trout dams, especially those at Kamberg and Cathedral Peak.

ABOVE Aeons ago, a boulder sculpted by nature tore itself free from a cliff of Giant's Castle, and rolled down the slope, erosion and lichens below transforming both its form and colours.

OPPOSITE Groves of mountain cypress have established themselves on the south-facing slope of the Mtshezana Stream at Champagne Pools close to the entrance of the Giant's Castle Game Reserve.

LEFT The robust – and rather common – tree fern (*Cyathea dregei*) is distributed throughout the Drakensberg region, often establishing itself in sinkholes along water courses and other moist depressions in grasslands and along forest margins.

BELOW Layers of Clarens sandstone provide welcome shelter for the wild poppie (*Papaver aculeatum*), which is relatively widespread among the boulder beds and under overhangs as high up in the Drakensberg as its alpine regions.

OPPOSITE Like all the rivers and streams of the Drakensberg, the Bushman's River (right) and Mtshezana Stream – pictured here at their confluence near the entrance of the Giant's Castle Game Reserve – play a major part in shaping the mountain scenery, hard at work transporting sediment, from the finest particle to the hugest boulder further and further downstream.

LEFT Jacobs Ladder, a small five-section waterfall within the confines of the Lotheni Mountain Reserve, is easy to reach and is thus a popular destination for family groups on picnic outings and other visitors to the 4000-hectare (9000-acre) valley reserve in the shadow of the high Drakensberg.

ABOVE The ancient cave of the famed Game Pass Shelter, alongside neighbouring Kamberg, protects one of the best sets of indigenous San rock art in the entire Berg.

OPPOSITE The approach to the Kamberg Mountain Reserve crosses the bottom end of the famous Game Pass, where soldiers of the 75th Natal Carbineer Regiment might have taken a wrong turn – their maps were far from reliable and knowledge of the Berg was still extremely limited in the 1870s. At the top of Giant's Castle, they stumbled into an ambush of local amaHlubi tribesmen led by Chief Langalibalele ('The Burning Sun'), who had dared defy the British colonial government of Natal.

The San cave paintings of Game Pass Shelter at Kamberg is not only regarded as one of the world's most remarkable rock-art sites by leading South African researchers, but is also one of the best preserved in southern Africa.

LEFT Most striking of the Game Pass Shelter's art are many multicoloured eland, which – as in many other paintings of its kind – superimposed over elongated human-like figures.

BELOW The colours of this panel are so vivid that it seems as though the painting was finished just recently, with the brush marks of the unknown artist still clearly visible.

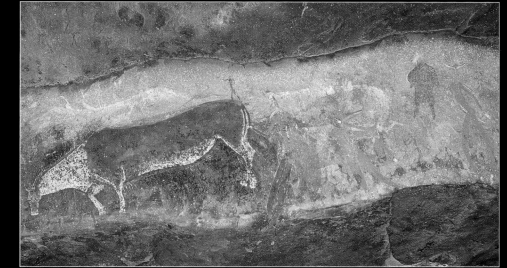

The images became known as the 'Rosetta Stone' panel as they provided a vital key that helped unlock much of the previously hidden meaning behind much of southern Africa's rock-art specimens or at least allowed researchers to interpret something of the mystery of San art, such as the close link between a dying eland and a San shaman in trance.

RIGHT In the centre of the Rosetta Stone, an eland, painted in white and reddish ochre, is apparently dying and is being watched by figures that are part human and part beast. It has been speculated that these are quite probably shamans immersed in a ritual trance, crossing the line between life and death.

LEFT The reflection of the towering heights of Giant's Castle is mirrored in one of the trout dams located in the picturesque, but little-known Highmoor Mountain Reserve.

TOP Highmoor Mountain Reserve, bordering on Giant's Castle Game Reserve, is not only a paradise for members of the trout-fishing fraternity, but one with an abundance of gentle vistas.

ABOVE The mountain slopes of the Highmoor reserve shelter a respectable population of eland, which are constantly under the threat of poaching so prevalent in this area.

OPPOSITE Highmoor is the only reserve in the Drakensberg were visitors can drive straight onto the top of the Little Berg and are able to admire the early morning atmosphere at leisure.

Opposite, clockwise from top left The lip-flower sugarbush (*Protea subvestita*); grass-leaved poker (*Kniphofia angustifolia*); *Crassula* species; the fairly dainty Drakensberg harebell (*Dierama dracomontanum*) is found at altitudes of about 2800 metres (6560 feet); the traveller's joy (*Clematis brachiata*) is traditionally used to treat snakebites, head colds and abdominal disorders, but takes its common name because it is said to act as a lucky charm.

This page, clockwise from top left The Drakensberg steekbos (*Metalasia densa*) helps brighten up surrounding Clarens sandstone; Cooper's aloe (*Aloe cooperi*) has edible flowers and leaves, and traditional healers recommend it to ensure pain-free childbirth; *Salvia fulgens* belongs to the large mint family and although many have healing powers, this invader from the Mediterranean or USA is quite useless and, fortunately, has not invaded the Berg as much as many others; the flowers of *Sebaea natalensis* may be used as a love charm; members of the *Erica* species are generally widespread and common in many parts of the Berg, where they are widely used by the Basotho people as fuel.

LEFT The pastoral Mkhomazi Mountain Reserve – bordered in the north by Giant's Castle and in the south by Sani Pass – is the largest, still untouched Wilderness Area of the Drakensberg.
BELOW The upper Mkhomazi River cuts through the conservation lands of the Vergelegen Mountain Reserve, but nevertheless arises in the huge Mkhomazi Wilderness Area.
BOTTOM Beyond the confines of the reserve that takes its name, the Mkhomazi River – also known as the Umkomaas – becomes broader and slower, much to the delight of local children.
OPPOSITE The road to Vergelegen – Dutch for 'far away' – winds through an extensive rural area in the mountain foothills, where most locals maintain a traditional way of life.

LEFT Although, on the face of it, fire is damaging to the environment, selective burning is an important part of the latter-day management of Berg reserves and wilderness areas

TOP Nervous blesbok stand at the ready to flee the controlled burning, introduced about 50 years ago to 'aid the conservation of biodiversity and avoid damage to soil structure'.

ABOVE Grassland of the Southern Berg burns to make for better environmental conditions.

OPPOSITE Although vital to the natural balance of the local ecology, even well-managed fires may spread out of control at an alarming rate. Here strong winds have dispersed the flames of a controlled fire between Kamberg and Giant's Castle, reaching Game Pass Shelter, where they have created golden hues – and endless headaches for local conservation staff.

OPPOSITE, CLOCKWISE FROM TOP LEFT This marsh Acraea (*Acraea rahira rahira*) is easily spotted at streams, rivers, dams and marshes; the best-known group of South Africa's several thousand spider species is the web-spinning spiders of the infraorder Araneomorphae; the pirate (*Catacroptera cloanthe*), on the wing all year, finds moisture in the droppings of a baboon; an African monarch (*Danaus chrysippus)* prefers the nectar offered by the spring flowers of a pompon tree; the *Potamonautes depressus* is the only crab species occurring in the Berg; dragonflies (*Anisoptera* sp.) are ever present at water sources in summer.

THIS PAGE, CLOCKWISE FROM TOP LEFT The grasslands of the Berg teem with grasshoppers of the family Acrididae, their hind legs adapted well to jumping. Most are very colourful, signalling with their brightly hued armour that they may be poisonous – much like the poisonous beetles of the family Melyridae (bottom left).

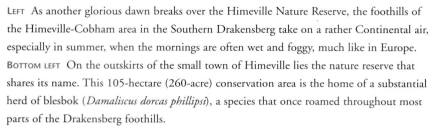

LEFT As another glorious dawn breaks over the Himeville Nature Reserve, the foothills of the Himeville-Cobham area in the Southern Drakensberg take on a rather Continental air, especially in summer, when the mornings are often wet and foggy, much like in Europe.

BOTTOM LEFT On the outskirts of the small town of Himeville lies the nature reserve that shares its name. This 105-hectare (260-acre) conservation area is the home of a substantial herd of blesbok (*Damaliscus dorcas phillipsi*), a species that once roamed throughout most parts of the Drakensberg foothills.

BELOW Although small herds of the irascible black wildebeest (*Connochaetes gnou*) may still be spotted in some Drakensberg reserves, there was a time when populations were severely threatened. By the end of the 19th century, the once-numerous species faced extinction, but conservation efforts as Golden Gate and other wildlife reserves served to turn the tide. Reintroductions into Giant's Castle Game Reserve and Royal Natal National Park were not, however, as successful.

OPPOSITE Because of the high quality of its soil and its favourable climate, which support both crop farming and cattle breeding, much of the land skirting the foothills of the Drakensberg have been cultivated. Yet, for the most part, the countryside has retained much of its appeal.

OPPOSITE, CLOCKWISE FROM LEFT Katstert (*Hebenstretia comosa*); the watsonia is widespread, with most of the 180-plus species native to southern Africa, although they are cultivated worldwide. They occur from open grassland to rocky areas high in the mountains, and help ensure good harvests; everlastings (*Helchrysum* sp.) are found in the higher Berg; flowers of the mostly succulent Crassula species vary from white to deep red-brown; everlastings at the Sentinel roadside.

THIS PAGE, CLOCKWISE FROM TOP LEFT Daisies of the *Berkheya* species are found at altitudes up to 2500 metres (8200 feet) and like moist grassy slopes and stream banks; the false scabiosa (*Cephalaria oblongifolia*) may form mats at up to 2800 metres (9200 feet); *Verbena tenuisecta* is another rather harmless intruder and tries to blend in with local species. It is a rather showy member of the mint and sage family, which has found its way from South African gardens into the Berg; *Hesperantha grandiflora* is a typical South African wild flower species of the iris family, and is best suited to heights of up to 3000 metres (9850 feet); the common gazania (*Gazania krebsiana*), whose flower heads close at night throughout the year, is also found at high altitudes

LEFT The perilous drive through Sani Pass to the distant Sani Top still appeals to the 4x4 motorist although it is now much easier to admire the mountain scenery and view from the top of the Escarpment than it was during the age of the mule train. The drive from the green foothills starts at about 1400 metres (5000 feet) and ends – after at least 14 hairpin bends – at the more desolate summit at a height of to 2873 metres (9426 feet).

ABOVE Although mountain biking is still in its infancy throughout the Berg, efforts are being made do promote the healthy, albeit strenuous and sometimes a little dangerous, pastime. Here, two intrepid cyclists bike down Sani Pass after crossing Lesotho on their sturdy mountain bikes.

OPPOSITE In December, a huge field of red-hot pokers (*Kniphofia* spp.) springs to life in the wetlands opposite the Twelve Apostles, an impressive buttress of peaks that guard the entrance to Sani Pass just before travellers reach the border post between South Africa and Lesotho.

TOP LEFT AND ABOVE When snow falls in the Drakensberg nearly everybody becomes a child again, revelling in the transformation of familiar surroundings into weird and wonderful shapes.

ABOVE The little Berg village of Himeville and its surrounds were transformed overnight by a thick blanket of snow and, much to the consternation of local villagers, the power supply and telephone lines to the outside world were broken.

LEFT Himeville's residents were less than happy about the fabulous winter wonderland when, for a day or two day, their village was completely snowbound.

OPPOSITE TOP Blesbok, in search of food in the Himeville Nature Reserve, battle to make their way through the deep layer of hard snow, frozen solid overnight.

OPPOSITE, BOTTOM LEFT Occasionally, the ice may crack under their weight, causing injury and almost certain death in the icy waters.

OPPOSITE, BOTTOM RIGHT Just a day after the snowfall, a few intrepid visitors return to the trout dams of the Himeville Nature Reserve – but by noon, with the sun beating down again, they have, surprisingly, already reached the day's bag limit.

LEFT The Garden Castle area is blessed with countless waterfalls and tranquil groves, but seldom is this more spectacular than along the Giant's Cup National Hiking Way, which constitutes a five-day trek – with the Escarpment nearly always in sight – through the foothills and the Little Berg from Sani Pass to Bushman's Nek.

BELOW The mountain cabbage tree (*Cussonia paniculata*) is a fairly common species along the Giant's Cup National Hiking Way, the Drakensberg's premier hiking trail. The fairly quick-growing tree, which is both frost and drought resistant, reaches about six metres (20 feet) in height and may be found at such high altitudes as 2000 metres (6560 feet).

OPPOSITE Between January and March, the strikingly beautiful scarlet river lily (*Schizostylis coccinea*) blooms on the stream bank of the Ngwangwane River, which has its source near the Sehlaba-Thebe National Park in Lesotho.

PREVIOUS PAGES Rolling hills, dramatic mountainscapes and countless dams and tarns distinguish the Garden Castle wilderness area, the southernmost section of the uKhahlamba Drakensberg Park, which ends at Bushman's Neck. The jagged battlements of Garden Castle were, in fact, for a brief period in 1835, known as Giant's Castle.

THIS PAGE, CLOCKWISE FROM TOP LEFT The creeping *Rhynchosia* species is used to treat rheumatism and headaches; the scarlet river lily (*Schizostylis coccinea*) occurs mostly at riverbanks; the leaves of the parasitic tall ink flower (*Harveya speciosa*) help treat black eyes and mental illness; Christmas bells (*Sandersonia aurantiaca*) may be used as an aphrodisiac or to scare the devil away; *Disa* species are ground orchids and are numerous in the Berg.

OPPOSITE, CLOCKWISE FROM TOP LEFT The scented yellow evening rose (*Oenothera stricta*) is actually a weed from Chile often used to ward off evil spirits and storms; the familiar red-hot poker; the butterfly lobelia (*Monopsis decipiens*) may treat rheumatism, skin disease and a running nose; the robust *Disa stachoides* orchids also help ward off evil spirits; *Sebaea natalensis* populate wetlands up to 2100 metres (6900 feet).

ABOVE Early explorers noted in their records and diaries a resemblance between the Garden Castle countryside and that of Edinburgh Castle.

OPPOSITE A small stream, tributary of the Ngwangwane River, meanders through the grass-green wetland of the upland grassveld in the southernmost KwaZulu-Natal Drakensberg.

LEFT The fertile farmland of the grassy Mzimkulu River Valley makes it ideal for stock farming.
TOP Although the foothills of the Southern Drakensberg, dominated by Hodgson's twin peaks, are now relatively peaceful, this was once the setting of a deadly drama in which the seriously injured Thomas Hodgson died during a violent thunderstorm, abandoned by his companions.
ABOVE A ferocious thunderstorm rages around Hodgson's Peaks where Thomas Hodgson still lies buried in undisturbed seclusion. The highest peaks south of Sani were once called Giant's Cup.
OPPOSITE Seen from the Cobham camp site, the mountain view of Cobham State Forest is dominated by Hodgson's Peaks and Masubasuba Pass, both engulfed by a heavy downpour.

LEFT AND BOTTOM LEFT The Drakensberg mountains of the northeastern Cape are known as the 'tail of the dragon'. Although it lacks the monumental rugged appeal of the 'back of the dragon' in KwaZulu-Natal, the region has a powerful attraction of its own. Here, the Barkly Pass Road links the towns of Elliot and Barkly East via a scenic drive.
BELOW As the sinking sun settles over the magnificent Karnmelkspruit Canyon near Lady Grey, the cliffs are bathed in fading light. The crags here are home to a sizeable colony of Cape vultures, while the waters host an ever-increasing population of trout.
OPPOSITE A gradient of 1:6 makes Joubert's Pass one of the steepest passes in South Africa. Built in 1914 by the Joubert family so that they were able to transport cheese to Lady Grey, the road winds about 50 kilometres (32 miles) through the mountainous Eastern Cape grasslands, which is emblazoned by a sea of wild flowers during spring.

Opposite A flight over the Southern Berg of KwaZulu-Natal reveals the considerable difference between the sandstone formations of its landscape compared to the shapes of Golden Gate on the other side of the mountains.

Above The Golden Gate Highlands National Park in the Free State is one of the finest places from which to admire and photograph the many variations of magnificent Clarens sandstone formations, originally known as 'cave sandstone'.

Right The familiar Brandwag Buttress is probably the most famous landmark of the Golden Gate Highlands National Park and, situated in the northeastern corner of the Free State Drakensberg, it stands in contrast to the mountain peaks of the KwaZulu-Natal Drakensberg.

Overleaf Following a heavy thunderstorm in the afternoon, night slowly descends on the Berg. Occasionally, a flash of lightning lights, like an afterthought, the deepening darkness.